Holiday in the Rain Forest

An Original Play

Holiday in the Rain Forest

An Original Play

by Douglas Love

HarperCollins*Publishers*

For Martha

Introduction

The first time I stepped inside a theater, I thought that it was the most magical place in the world. I went with my class to see a show at the performing arts center in my town. It was a musical for children produced by a professional company of actors. I was immediately captivated. Right there in front of me, performers were singing and dancing and telling a story—live! It seemed that they were talking directly to me, and I was completely enthralled with the characters and their adventures. The sets and costumes weren't fancy or extravagant, but this made me even more involved in the production. I was able to use my imagination to pick up where the limitations of the sets and costumes left off. This first production was my introduction to the world of theater.

You are about to embark on an exciting adventure. Planning, rehearsing, and staging a play can be a fun and satisfying experience. It's up to you to make your play the best it can be. The written script is only the beginning. It is meant to be used like a map, a route that guides you through the story.

Because actors in a play are right in front of an audience (not up on a movie screen or inside a television), anything can happen, and it usually does. Scenery may fall over, people may say the wrong lines at the wrong time or forget their lines altogether. When these mistakes happen, the actors can't stop and start over. In the theater, they go right on and try to get back on track with as much ease as possible. This is the challenge of live theater. The feeling that *anything can happen* keeps everyone on their toes.

While working on your production, don't be discouraged if you feel that you don't have the exact prop or costume that the play calls for. If the stage directions ask for a couch in a certain scene, there is no rule that says you can't use a bench, or a chair, or nothing at all instead. You should decide what you think is important to include. Some of the best plays have no props or stage settings at all. The audience has to use its imagination, which can be a lot of fun.

It is almost always helpful to have someone serve as the director of the play, whether you are performing in your school or your backyard. This person will help make decisions about the direction your production takes: Will everyone wear costumes? Will you make a set? Who will play which character? He or she may also designate certain parts of the stage to be different places where the action takes place. The director should also help everyone working on the play realize that theater is a collaborative art. This means that the talents of a lot of people come together to create one exciting production that everyone can be proud of because everyone helped to create it.

Performers have a special task in the play. When you know what role you will play, the next step is to develop your character. This is achieved by asking yourself a lot of questions: If I was this person (or animal), how would I walk? How would I stand? How would I speak? What would I wear? Whom do I like in the play? Whom don't I like? What do I want to do in the play? You can and should ask yourself these and more questions about your character. Then, you have to answer these questions and make some decisions. If you are playing an old man, you might decide to stand hunched over and walk with a cane. You may choose to have a gravelly voice and tattered clothes. You may discover while reading the play that you are a rich old man who doesn't spend any of his money, and you are afraid that everyone is trying to steal it.

The answers and decisions that you make about your character are guideposts on your journey. It's okay to change your mind if something isn't working. None of the choices that you make for your character are wrong. Experiment! That's what rehearsals are for. Refer to the performance tips before each play for some suggestions.

Rehearsal is extremely important if you plan to perform your play for an audience. Some theater directors and actors believe that you should rehearse one hour for every minute that you are onstage. Some of that rehearsal time can be spent on your own, memorizing your lines. Different people memorize lines differently, but all techniques have one thing in common— repetition. Go over and over and over your lines until you can say them without looking at the script. Some people sit alone reading their lines again and again until they can say them from memory. Others read their lines into a tape recorder and listen to the tape over and over. Or ask a friend or someone in your family to "hold book." This means that they read the line that comes before yours and then you say your line.

Rehearsal is also the time to decide on your blocking, or the physical action of the play. Who does what, when? If everything is planned before the performance, you'll feel more secure, and the audience will be able to follow the story more easily.

When planning your blocking, remember that you are performing for an audience that needs to see what is going on to follow the story of the play. Important action should take place closer to the audience. Try to face the audience as much as possible; this allows them to see your facial expressions and hear you better.

Whether you will be performing on your school stage, in your classroom, or at home, feel free to make changes to make the play work for you, and use them as a jumping off point into the unlimited world of your own creativity and imagination.

About *Holiday in the Rain Forest*

You'll want to keep the following performance tips in mind if you're putting on your own production of *Holiday in the Rain Forest*.

The Characters

The following descriptions of the characters in *Holiday in the Rain Forest* are just a starting point. It is up to you to fully develop your own character by reading the play carefully, and forming your own opinion of your character's personality.

Frannie Kane is the mom in the Kane family. At first she wants to show off and impress her friends. She eventually learns that there are more important things than showing off vacation slides.

Manny Kane is the dad in the Kane family. Like his wife, he comes to realize there is more to a trip than fancy souvenirs.

Anne Kane is Frannie and Manny's 11-year-old daughter. She likes to figure things out for herself.

Gilbert Kane is Frannie and Manny's 10-year-old son. He is often bored—until he gets to the rain forest.

Ray is the multipersonality worker at the rain forest motel. Every time he changes his hat and becomes someone else, he should also change the way that he stands, moves, and talks!

Gladys Montrose lives with her husband and children near the Kanes. She is very concerned with outdoing her neighbors.

George Montrose is Gladys's husband. He is also very concerned with appearances and material things.

Ginny and **Winny Montrose** are George and Gladys's twin daughters. They are spoiled and are constantly arguing.

Spike Montrose is the Montroses' baby. Spike is very demanding and loud.

Jack and **Melvin** are wisecracking, good-hearted alligators. They are like an old-fashioned comedy team. They laugh at each other's jokes harder than anyone else, even though they have already heard the jokes many times.

Rontihowa and **Antelo** are stone people who are very sensitive and caring. When they are brought back to life, they are full of wonder about their environment.

Ti is a tiny, beautiful butterfly. Ti cares about the stone people and genuinely wants to help them.

Chris Dayton, the talk-show host, is overly perky and full of smiles.

Sets and Props

As you read through the play, a picture will form in your mind of how a certain scene looks. Think about this picture, and how you can re-create it onstage through sets and props. The goal of sets and props is to give the audience a feeling for where the action is taking place.

Be observant. Pay close attention to things around you. What are five things that make your family's living room look like a living room? Use your imagination! How do you think a rain forest would look? What props can you add or take away to make the Kanes' living room look very different from the lobby of Ray's Rain Forest

Motel and Emporium?

Holiday in the Rain Forest takes place in a few different locations. There are two different living rooms, the Kanes' and the Montroses'. The Montroses' might have pictures on their walls or souvenirs that they've purchased on their vacations. Set up different configurations of chairs and tables to distinguish the two living-room areas. You might want to use the same furniture with different blankets or covers draped over them for the two different houses. If the furniture isn't arranged differently for the different houses, the audience might get confused.

The lobby of Ray's Rain-Forest Motel and Emporium should have a desk that is large enough so the audience cannot see Ray when he ducks behind it. The desk should be cluttered with papers and office supplies.

The last scene takes place on the set of a television talk show. The characters should be sitting in a row of chairs across the stage, with Chris, the talk-show host, either standing or sitting on one end in a larger chair. She might carry a fake microphone.

Other props that you may need to include are telephones for the Kanes' and Montroses' living rooms, a camera, and four sleeping bags.

Costumes

It's fun to pretend that you are somebody else in a play. When you add the element of costume and you begin to look like a character and not like yourself, the fun really begins.

Following is a description of what each character might wear. Remember that these are only suggestions. Feel free to be creative. Don't be discouraged if you don't have the exact costume described. It's fun to look for the costume that you feel comfortable wearing as the character!

When the Kanes open their suitcases at Ray's Rain Forest Motel and Emporium, they find torn, simple tunics instead of their own clothes. You can make these tunics by draping an old sheet or a piece of cloth over your shoulders and tying it around your waist with rope or a belt. If you decide to cut holes in the sheet for your head and arms, make sure you ask your parents first.

Frannie Kane wears a coat for her first entrance and then takes it off to reveal a skirt, a shirt, and maybe a string of pearls. She might also wear earrings and shoes with heels to make her look older. When she is in the rain forest she wears a ragged tunic.

Manny Kane also wears a coat in his first entrance. When he takes it off, he is wearing a colorful shirt and pants. He wears a ragged tunic in the rain forest.

Anne Kane wears frilly clothes. She also wears a ragged tunic for her adventure in the rain forest.

Gilbert Kane probably wears jeans and a T-shirt. When he is in the rain forest, he should wear a ragged tunic.

Ray needs a different hat for each of the jobs he covers. Or he might use the same hat for each character but with different name tags attached.

Gladys Montrose might wear a skirt, a blouse, and simple jewelry.

George Montrose's clothes were influenced by his trip to Mexico. He might wear a red shirt, black pants, and a large sombrero. Over his shirt he could wear a poncho.

Ginny Monorose and **Winny Montrose** are twins and dress exactly alike.

Spike Montrose might be dressed in baby pajamas and possibly a leather jacket. He could have a pacifier or something else that shows he's a baby.

Jack and **Melvin** should be dressed in greens and browns. They might have tails of stuffed material, which you can attach to a belt, and sunglasses or fun green hats.

Rontihowa and **Antelo** might be dressed in gray tunics. When they come to life they can take off their tunics to reveal more colorful clothes.

Ti should have colorful wings made out of construction paper or fabric that flow when her arms move. She could also wear a colorful leotard and tights.

Chris Dayton might wear a blazer and skirt or a woman's business suit.

Cast

Frannie Kane
Manny Kane
Anne Kane
Gilbert Kane
Ray
Gladys Montrose
George Montrose
Winny Montrose
Ginny Montrose
Spike Montrose
Jack, an alligator
Melvin, an alligator
Ti, a butterfly
Rontihowa, a stone person
Antelo, a stone person
Chris Dayton, a talk-show host

Optional Smaller Cast
Actor 1—Frannie Kane, Winny Montrose
Actor 2—Manny Kane
Actor 3—Anne Kane, Ginny Montrose
Actor 4—Gilbert Kane
Actor 5—Chris Dayton, Ti, Spike Montrose
Actor 6—George Montrose, Melvin, Antelo, Ray
Actor 7—Gladys Montrose, Jack, Rontihowa

Setting

Scene 1

★ *We are inside the* KANES' *house. The stage is set to be a living room. A couch is placed on an angle left of center stage. A chair right of center faces the couch. There is a table with a lamp, phone, and answering machine. There are plastic food bags and empty soda cans spread throughout the set. The front door is offstage left.*

★ FRANNIE KANE, *a woman in her forties who is very concerned about what other people think, enters.* MANNY KANE, FRANNIE's *husband, also in his forties, enters with* FRANNIE. *Both are wearing hats, coats, and scarves.*

Frannie: That's it! *(fuming as she crosses to the couch)* That Gladys Montrose makes me so mad!

Manny *(taking off his coat)*: I can't ever remember being so bored in my life.

Frannie *(taking off her coat)*: The way they carried on!

Manny: Couldn't get a word in edgewise.

Frannie: How could they possibly think that we enjoyed ourselves this evening?

Manny: Is that their idea of entertaining?

Frannie: Is that their idea of a relaxing evening with friends?

Both *(together)*: Vacation slides!

Frannie *(mimicking)*: Pedro was our guide to the ancient city.

Manny *(also mimicking)*: The food was top rate, can't get anything like it in the States.

Frannie: Then when she started speaking with an accent and rolling her Rs!

Manny: And when he took out that big hat and started to dance!

Both *(together)*: WHAT A BORE! *(long pause)*

Frannie *(looking around the room)*: Will you

look at this place? Those kids! It looks like a tornado hit.

Manny: I'll clean it up, dear. *(He gets up to clean. FRANNIE remains on the couch.)* Where are the paper bags?

Frannie: Oh, I throw those away. I have some plastic bags in the corner, there.

★ *MANNY begins to pick up garbage, throwing it into the plastic bag.*

Manny: What about these cans? Should I separate them?

Frannie: Separate them? They all end up in the same place! *(thinking)* Don't they? *(thinking more)* Honey? Where does all of this garbage end up, anyway?

Manny: In the garbage truck!

Frannie: Oh, of course! I almost forgot.

★ *MANNY continues to pick up garbage and place it all into one bag.*

Frannie: Honey? Why don't we take the kids to Mexico?

Manny: We just went on vacation!

Frannie: Just went? Where?

Manny: That amusement park with the rides and cartoon characters walking around.

Frannie: Amusement park?! You mean the rocking horse in the parking lot of the A & P with the bag boys who have to wear duck costumes?

Manny: The kids loved it.

Frannie: Gilbert threw up all over Dippy the Duck.

Manny: But he had fun!

Frannie: More than I can say for the duck. Oh, Manny, let's go away. What I wouldn't give to bore Gladys and George with our slides.

Manny: I think I've got some shots of Dippy.

Frannie: Please, Manny? Let's take the kids somewhere exotic.

Manny: Where?

Frannie: It has to be a place that none of our friends have gone.

Manny: I'm not going to the North Pole!

Frannie: Oh, no . . . the Jeffersons went there last Christmas. Now let's see, we can't go to Greece. The Andropolises went to Greece.

Manny: Italy?

Frannie: No, the Jorgensons went to Italy.

Manny: Ireland?

Frannie: The Peabodys went to Ireland.

Manny: China?

Frannie: No, no! The Georges had Sara's sweet sixteen in China. *(pause)* I know. . . Brazil! Oh, yes! Brazil! That's perfect! We could take trips into the wilderness! We could really "rough it"!

Manny: I'll pick up some travel books tomorrow!

★ *Blackout*

Scene 2

★ *Same location the next night. FRANNIE is looking through a brochure. MANNY is on the telephone.*

Manny *(on the phone)*: Hello? . . . Hello?! Is this Ray's Rain Forest Motel and Emporium? *(pause)* It is? Oh, great! Great! Now, are you located right in the heart of the rain forest? *(pause)* You're not? How far? *(pause)* A forty-five minute hike?

Frannie *(getting excited)*: Hike? Oh, a hike! *(calling offstage)* Did you hear that, kids? We're going to hike!

Manny: Yes. There are four of us, and the name is Kane. Now, we really want to "rough it"! We're looking for an adventure, or at least some really good photo opportunities! We'll be there Thursday! Good-bye.

Frannie: This is too much! Too much! Wait until I tell Gladys Montrose that we're going to the rain forest of South America! *(She crosses to the phone,* *then stops herself.)* No! I'll let them call us and get the answering machine!

Manny *(yelling offstage)*: Kids! Are you all packed?

★ *ANNE, eleven years old, enters wearing a frilly dress.*

Anne *(entering the stage from her room)*: Pretty much. Should I pack a dress?

Manny: A dress? No, honey, we're "roughing it"!

Frannie: You never know, dear. Maybe you'll need a dress. They may have a nice restaurant at the motel. After all, it is an emporium!

Manny: Then I better take a tie and jacket.

Frannie *(calling offstage to GILBERT)*: Gilbert, make sure you pack a tie!

★ *GILBERT, ten years old, is dressed in jeans, T-shirt, and sneakers.*

Gilbert *(entering from his room, carrying a big stack of newspapers)*: Do I have to?

Frannie: Yes, dear, you have to. Honestly!

Gilbert: Mom, what should I do with all of these newspapers I used for my social-studies project?

Frannie: Just throw them in with the garbage. I don't want them cluttering up the house! Get rid of them.

Anne: Mom, should I pack a raincoat?

Frannie: Oh, no, dear. "Rain" forest is just a figure of speech. It doesn't actually rain there.

★ *Blackout*

Scene 3

★ *The lobby of Ray's Rain Forest Motel and Emporium. There is a chair downstage left and a motel check-in desk upstage right. RAY, the motel owner, enters. Each time the KANES ask to speak to someone else, RAY ducks behind the desk and changes his hat to become the new character.*

★ *RAY walks behind the check-in desk and disappears behind it.*

★ *FRANNIE, MANNY, ANNE, and GILBERT enter completely drenched from the rain.*

Anne: I am completely soaked!

Gilbert *(shivering)*: I'm freezing!

Manny *(mimicking FRANNIE)*: "Rain" forest is just a figure of speech!

Frannie: So I made a mistake! You've never made a mistake? Besides, we've just had our very first experience in "roughing it."

Manny: Mom's right, kids. Now we're at the motel. We can dry off and change our clothes. I'll check us in.

★ *MANNY walks over to the check-in desk and rings the service bell. RAY pops up from behind the desk.*

Ray: Hello. I'm Ray, the desk clerk. Welcome to Ray's Rain Forest Motel and Emporium. How may I help you?

Manny: We have reservations. Our name is Kane.

Ray *(looking through stacks of disorganized papers)*: Hmm. Kane, Kane. *(to MANNY)* Kane?

Manny: Yes, Kane.

Ray *(back to his papers)*: Hmm. Kane, Kane.

Manny *(becoming impatient)*: I don't understand this! We made the reservation just last week.

Frannie *(crossing to MANNY)*: Is there something wrong?

Manny: This guy can't find our reservation.

Frannie: What do you mean, he can't find our reservation? You made it last week. I heard you. *(to RAY)* I heard him!

Manny: Who's in charge here?

Ray: That would be Ray, the manager.

Manny: Then, I want to speak with Ray the manager.

★ *RAY ducks down behind the desk and reappears wearing a new hat.*

Ray: Can I help you folks?

Manny: No, no. We'll wait for the manager.

Ray: I am the manager. My name is Ray. Can I help you?

Manny: You're the manager?

Ray: Yes.

Manny: Why didn't you say that before?

Ray: Before what?

Manny: Before, when we first tried to check in.

Ray: That was Ray, the desk clerk. He told me that you folks needed my assistance.

Manny: Ray the desk clerk?

Ray: Yes.

Frannie: You're Ray the manager?

Ray: Yes . . . and your name?

★ *FRANNIE and MANNY look at each other and shrug.*

Manny: The name's Kane.

Ray *(looking through the papers)*: Kane. . . Kane . . . No. No Kane listed. Sorry.

Frannie: We have to be listed. We just called last week!

Ray: You called last week? Well, then. That explains it!

Manny: Explains what?

Ray: Ray, the new guy, was answering the phone last week.

Frannie: Ray the new guy?

Ray: Just hired him. He was messing up everything! Hold on, I'll get him. *(He ducks under the desk to retrieve a new hat, and emerges as RAY the new guy.)* Hi! I'm Ray the new guy. Ray the manager said that you needed my help?

Manny: You're Ray the new guy?

Frannie: You're Ray the new guy?

Ray: Wow! I never realized that there was an echo in here! Ray said you guys called last week? What's your name?

Manny *(running out of patience)*: KANE.

Ray: Let's just take a little look in the file.

Manny: They've already looked in the file and we're not there.

Ray *(finding the piece of paper)*: Here you are, under "L."

Frannie: "L"?

Ray: For "Last week"!

Manny: We don't care! We've been traveling all day. We are drenched and very tired. Which room are we in?

Ray: Which room? We've only got one room.

Frannie: One room? Is it vacant?

Ray: Sure it is. Nobody's ever stayed here. Not many people come to the rain forest for vacation. I'll call Ray the bellboy to get your bags. *(He gets another hat to become RAY the bellboy.)* Hello, sir. Which room are you in?

Manny: You've only got one room!

Ray: But of course. This way please.

★ *He leads the family offstage.*

★ *Blackout*

29

Scene 4

★ *The motel room at Ray's Rain Forest Motel and Emporium.* RAY *leads* FRANNIE, MANNY, GILBERT, *and* ANNE *to an empty room with sleeping bags rolled up in the center.*

Ray: Here you are. Home away from home!

Frannie: Your brochure said "lovely, spacious rooms."

Ray: You have to admit, there's lots of room in here!

Manny: That's because there's no furniture.

Gilbert: Where's the bathroom?

Ray: Well, do you see that tree over there?

Frannie *(looking out the window)*: Yes.

Ray: Turn left.

Manny: Now that's "roughing it."

Ray: Well, folks, my day's done. I'm going home. If you need anything . . .

Frannie: Let me guess. . . Ray the night clerk, right?

Ray: Oh, no. Pops watches the place at night. If you need anything, just ask him. He'll help you out. Good night.

★ *RAY exits.*

Anne: I don't like this place.

Gilbert: I want to go home.

Frannie: Now, kids, this is our family adventure. Our hotel room may not be fancy, but we've come here to "rough it." At least we have a room. Now, let's unpack and change into some dry clothes and go to bed.

Anne *(opening a suitcase)*: This isn't our stuff.

Frannie: What do you mean, this isn't our stuff? *(She looks at the clothes.)* Manny, this isn't our stuff.

Manny *(opening another suitcase)*: We must have picked up the wrong bags.

Frannie: Well, we have to get out of these wet clothes.

Gilbert *(taking a tunic-style costume out of one suitcase)*: These clothes look weird.

Manny: This must be what people wear around here.

Frannie: Just think of the great pictures we can take in these.

Manny: Okay, everybody. Change and go to bed. We've got a big day of pictures tomorrow.

Frannie: I'd give anything to see Gladys Montrose's face when she hears that we are vacationing in the South American rain forest!

★ *Blackout*

Scene 5

★ *The Montrose home.* GLADYS, *a woman in her late
thirties, is on the phone.* GEORGE, *her husband,
also late thirties, is reading the paper. With each
page he finishes, he crinkles it up and puts it in a
plastic bag.* SPIKE, *the baby, is in his playpen.*

Gladys: The South American what? George!
George!

George: What is it, Gladys?

Gladys: Frannie and Manny are in the South
American rain forest on vacation!

George: Big deal!

Gladys: That means that next year we'll have to
go on some sort of safari.

George: If I know them, they'll want to show off
and invite us to see some boring vacation slides
when they get back.

Gladys: That would be just like them.

★ *WINNY enters with GINNY, her twin. Both are twelve years old and dressed alike.*

Winny: Mommy, Ginny stepped on my Italian shoes that we got on our trip to Rome last year, and got them all dirty.

Ginny: Not before she stepped on my Mexican hat that we got from our vacation in Cancun.

George: Now you two go back to bed on your Swedish mattresses that we got on our vacation to Stockholm and wrap yourselves up in your Egyptian blankets that we got on our vacation to Cairo and go to sleep.

Ginny: That blanket makes me itch!

Gladys: It's not your blanket that itches. It's your yak-wool pajamas that we got you on our vacation to Tibet.

Ginny: Do I have to wear them?

George: Of course you do. They're a souvenir.

Winny: Mommy, did you find out where Anne and Gilbert went?

Gladys: Yes, dear. They went with their parents to the South American rain forest!

Winny: What's a rain forest?

George: It's sort of like a jungle.

Spike: Go to the rain forest! Go to the rain forest!

Ginny: Will they see real animals there?

Spike: See real animals! See real animals!

Winny: Why don't we ever go anywhere fun for vacation?

Spike: Go somewhere fun! Go somewhere fun!

Gladys *(impatiently)*: Spike, please! We go to lots of fun places!

Winny: Daddy, please let us come along to see the slides of the rain forest.

Spike: See slides! See slides!

George *(worn down)*: Okay, you can see the slides!

Gladys: Now, everyone go to bed! *(The twins help* SPIKE *out of the playpen and the three kids exit.)* If I know Frannie and Manny, they are probably in a fancy, beautiful hotel with lots of servants and nice restaurants.

George: That's the difference between us. If we were there, we'd really want to get a feel for things. We'd really "rough it."

★ *Blackout*

Scene 6

★ *The outskirts of the rain forest. The Kane family enters, stage left. They come upon two alligators, JACK and MELVIN.*

Anne *(to the alligators)*: Excuse me, we're looking for the rain forest. Do you know how to get there?

Jack *(teasing)*: The rain forest? GET IN LINE! *(to MELVIN)* You hear that, Melvin? These folks are looking for the rain forest!

Melvin *(laughing)*: The rain forest? What makes you think you can find the rain forest? Sitting here in this swamp, we see it all.

Jack: Last night, Melvin and I met a guy who was looking for the fountain of youth.

Melvin: Give it up. There's a broken dream for every lily pad on the swamp.

Frannie: Excuse me? Mister Alligator? Would

you mind posing for a picture with my son?

Gilbert *(embarrassed)*: Ma!

Manny: Go on, son! It'll be cute.

Melvin: Now, pictures I do! How do I look, Jack?
Do I got any people stuck between my teeth?

★ *The family freezes in shock.*

Melvin: Just kidding!

★ *They all laugh nervously.*

Manny *(focusing the camera)*: Now, Gilbert, you
get right in there with the alligator. Wait till
Gladys and George see this one! Okay! Look
fierce. *(He snaps the picture.)* Great shot!

Jack: All right, you got your picture, now go home!

Frannie: We can't go home! There are too many
photo opportunities that we would miss. Besides,
we've come a long way to see the rain forest.

Jack: Give me a break! Yeah, the rain forest used

to come all the way out to this swamp. I guess that technically you are in the rain forest right now.

Anne: This isn't a forest. There aren't any trees here.

Melvin: Oh, this place was full of trees, once upon a time.

Manny: Once upon a time?

Melvin: They came through here and cut down all the trees around this swamp.

Gilbert: Why?

Jack: Farmers want the land, kid.

Frannie: Will the trees grow back?

Melvin: Trees don't grow back overnight. They haven't even replanted, and I'm not sure that they're planning to. To find the trees, you'll have to go near the mountains.

Manny *(looking at his map)*: . . . and beyond the valleys?

Jack: You are already beyond the valleys.

Melvin: The mountains are far away. You have to travel on to see them.

Jack: Come with us. We will take you to the mountains.

Gilbert: Let's go!

★ *They move across the stage to the area that is at the edge of the mountains.*

Jack: Here we are. This is beyond the valleys and near the mountains.

★ *They all look around and see that there are still no trees.*

Frannie: There aren't any trees here either.

Melvin: They must have cut or burned these down, too.

Jack: They must be printing a lot of newspapers for you guys, with those trees.

Frannie: They aren't using these trees to make paper products that we use at home! We live very far from here.

Melvin: The paper made from the trees in the rain forest gets shipped all over the world.

Jack: Maybe there are some trees on the other side of the mountains. We can lead you to the edge of the swamp, but you're on your own after that.

★ *They all exit.*

★ *Blackout*

Scene 7

★ *The Land of the Stone People. The family comes across what appear to be statues of people. Two actors are standing centerstage, resembling statues. They wear drab gray-and-brown tunics and stand very still.*

Frannie *(yelling offstage to the alligators)*: Thanks! Take care!

Manny *(waving his camera)*: We'll send you copies of the snapshots!

Frannie: Bye!

Manny *(looking at all of the statues)*: WHAT IS THIS?

Gilbert: They look like statues.

Frannie: They don't look like any of the ancient heroes that I read about in the tour books.

Anne: Something is written on the side here.

Manny: What is it? What does it say?

Anne *(reading a small plaque next to* ANTELO *and* RONTIHOWA*)*: "Lost their hope—turned to stone."

Frannie *(puzzled)*: Lost their hope—turned to stone? What does that mean? *(She looks at* MANNY *and smiles.)* Picture time!

★ *They all gather around a stone person while* MANNY *focuses.*

Gilbert: Look at this one! *(pointing to a statue)* Look at its eyes. They look very human.

Anne: You don't think these are people who have turned to stone, do you?

Frannie: Don't be silly! It is the artist's job to make the statue look real.

Gilbert: Well, this artist did a great job. This one is blinking!

Anne: Let's get out of here!

★ *They start to exit.* FRANNIE *stops them.*

Frannie: This is crazy! Statues don't blink!

★ *They look more closely at the statues.* MANNY *looks at his map.*

Gilbert: These statues are spooky. *(Looks closely at one of them.)* Their eyes look very lifelike. *(One of the stone people blinks.)* Did you see that?

Anne: See what?

Gilbert: That one! He moved his eyes!

★ *They all rush over.*

Manny *(to* ANTELO*)*: Can you hear us? Do you understand us?

★ ANTELO *blinks again, trying to communicate.*

Frannie *(to* ANTELO*)*: Are you alive? *(to* MANNY*)* He's moving his eyes—but he can't communicate with us! These are people, Manny! They're not statues!

44

Anne *(rereading the plaque)*: It says here, "Lost their hope—turned to stone." What could that mean, "Lost their hope"? I wonder what happened?

★ *Suddenly,* TI, *a butterfly, enters.*

Ti *(to* MANNY*)*: Hello.

Manny: Hello. Who are you?

Ti: I'm Ti. I'm a butterfly.

Frannie *(in a loud voice, as if* TI *doesn't understand English)*: GREETINGS! I AM FRANNIE. THIS IS MY HUSBAND, MANNY, AND OUR CHILDREN, GILBERT AND ANNE.

Ti: What are you doing here among these stones?

Anne *(to* TI*)*: These are people who have turned to stone!

Ti: Turned to stone? How did that happen?

Gilbert: We don't know. There's only this little

sign here that says, "Lost their hope—turned to stone."

Ti: "Lost their hope"? What does that mean?

Anne: That was my question.

Frannie: Maybe if we gathered some fruits and berries and tried to feed them, they would come back to life.

Manny: Let's try it.

Anne: We have berries that we gathered on the trail up here with the alligators.

★ *They all take some of the fruits and berries from* ANNE *and try feeding* RONTIHOWA *and* ANTELO. *Nothing happens.*

Ti: It doesn't work. They're as stiff as they were when we began.

Gilbert *(thinking)*: "Lost their hope." Hmm. I wonder.

Ti: I have an idea. *(running off)* I'll be right back!

Anne: Where's she going?

Manny: I don't know. Look at her fly! Her wings are so beautiful and colorful.

Frannie *(looking up into the sky)*: Look, she's bringing others. Look at all those colors!

★ *The actors onstage look up above the heads of the audience and pretend to see the butterflies and birds. They focus on the imaginary birds and butterflies until* RONTIHOWA *and* ANTELO *slowly come back to life.* RONTIHOWA *and* ANTELO *slowly begin to move their heads, then arms, and finally legs.*

Rontihowa: You have saved us. All of you! I am Rontihowa, and this is Antelo. We wish to express our gratitude.

Frannie: We're glad to help.

Manny: How did you lose your hope? What does that mean? What happened?

Antelo: We used to be a joyful, contented people. We lived in harmony with all of the plants and

47

creatures of the rain forest. Then some strangers came in with big machines that cut up our beautiful trees. Many animals lost their homes and became very sick. When we lost our trees, our hearts turned cold and gray with grief and despair.

Frannie: That's terrible.

Antelo: This area was once filled with trees and plants and animals. They cleared the entire area.

Rontihowa: When our hearts turned cold and hard, the rest of us turned to stone as well.

Antelo: When we saw the lively beauty and color of the butterflies and birds, our hearts turned warm and our skin soft again. With beautiful colors like that, it makes us feel that there may be some hope again. How can we ever thank you?

Manny: Your turning from stone is thanks enough. We hope to come back and visit you one day, but right now we are going to find the rain forest.

Frannie: Please tell us where you live so we can send you a postcard.

Rontihowa: We used to live among the trees. We no longer have a home.

Anne: Then you must come with us! You will help us find the rain forest, and we will help you to make sure that the trees there are never cut down.

Manny *(consulting his map)*: Let's look on the other side of the mountains.

★ *They all follow* MANNY *offstage.*

★ *Blackout*

Scene 8

★ *Further into the rain forest. The group enters the stage.*

Frannie *(pointing out to the audience)*: Look, everyone! The river! Look at it! It's beautiful. All of the rivers back home are brown and polluted.

Anne and **Gilbert** *(amazed, looking out at the river)*: Wow!

Manny: Look at all the plants and trees!

Rontihowa: This is the perfect spot! We can rebuild our homes with respect for all of nature living together.

Manny: How can people cut down these beautiful trees? We have to tell everyone back home about this place and how important it is that all living things—people, animals, trees, and plants—live together with respect. It's up to us. Humans are the only ones who can make a difference. Where's the camera, honey?

Frannie: I gave it to Gilbert.

Gilbert: I don't have it. I gave it to Anne.

Anne: Me? I never get to hold the camera. Dad is always afraid I'm going to drop it.

Gilbert: Well, don't look at me. I don't have it.

Manny: This is just great! We have this adventure and we have nothing to show for it!

Frannie: Oh, yes we do! Just look around. This is what we have to show! We can make a difference. We can help!

Gilbert: How can we help from all the way back home?

Frannie: Well, they say that the trees are cut down to make paper goods. If we start to recycle our paper, maybe they won't need to cut down so many new trees. And if we do our part, maybe people all over the world will pitch in and do their part as well. Pictures and showing off to neighbors, that's silly. What is important is the rain forest and all of its creatures!

★ *Blackout*

Scene 9

★ *The set of* The Chris Dayton Show. CHRIS DAYTON
enters with a microphone. GLADYS *and* GEORGE
MONTROSE *and* FRANNIE *and* MANNY KANE *are
seated in chairs placed on the stage.* CHRIS *might
take her place in the audience, as on a TV talk
show. She pretends that the audience for the
play is also the audience for her talk show.*

Chris: If you're just joining us, today we're talking
travel. Vacations. Family vacations! Surveys say
that more than fifty-six percent of you are traveling
with your kids. Is it worth it? We're going to find
out! Meet the Kanes and the Montroses. Both
families have recently returned from vacations.

★ GLADYS *and* GEORGE *are very excited. The* KANES
look calm and relaxed.

Gladys: Pedro was our guide to the ancient city.

George: The food was top rate! Can't get
anything like it in the States.

53

Gladys: You know, when they talk, they roll their Rs. *(demonstrating)* Like *r*ed *r*obin *r*ocket! Isn't that cute?

George: I got some great slides of this dance they do around a hat! They actually put a hat on the ground and stomp around it! Don't ya just love it?

Chris *(to the KANES)*: Mr. and Mrs. Kane. You took your family to the South American rain forest. That must have been very exciting. I'm sure you have stories that would put all the experiences we heard about today to shame.

★ *The KANES look at each other.*

Frannie: What's a shame is the state of the rain forest. We could hardly find it.

Manny: People are cutting down all the trees.

Frannie: Did you know there is a recycling program that we have right here in our town? We never even knew about it!

Manny: We do now!

Frannie: Did you know that if everyone in the U.S. recycled their Sunday newspapers, we could save five hundred thousand trees a week here at home!

Manny: That's twenty-six million a year! If we do our part, maybe other countries will do their part, too. Then we might not lose so many trees. And the rain forest might become a home to many living creatures once again.

Chris: What about the vacation? Any slides? Was it as wonderful as the Montroses' vacation?

Manny: No slides this trip.

Frannie: Just tourist traps and high prices. We wouldn't recommend it as a vacation spot.

★ *FRANNIE and MANNY look at each other and smile.*

★ *Blackout*

★ *Curtain*

Douglas Love began his career in theater as a child actor and grew up in show business, appearing in more than fifty productions. He has produced five national tours in more than seventy cities across the United States. Mr. Love is the author of *Be Kind to Your Mother (Earth)*, *Blame It on the Wolf*, and *Kabuki Gift*, all published by HarperCollins. He is also the coauthor of the stage adaptation of *Free to Be . . . You and Me*. Mr. Love is on the faculty of The Children's Theater School in Milwaukee, Wisconsin, and is a guest teacher at the school's Summer Theater Workshop in Vail, Colorado. Douglas Love lives in New York City.